A Practical Guide to Drugs and Alcohol Testing

Everything you ever wanted to know about
drugs & alcohol testing but were afraid to ask

by

Dr Dan Hegarty and Mike Stallard

Grosvenor House
Publishing Limited

Dr Dan Hegarty studied at St Edmund Hall (Oxford University) and Guy's Hospital Medical School (London University). He qualified as a doctor in 1985 and has worked in occupational health since 1996. His professional interests include occupational drugs & alcohol screening and testing.

Mike Stallard is an independent business consultant. He was previously a senior manager in the rail industry where he gained extensive experience in corporate management. During the past ten years Mike has worked in the field of occupational health and drugs screening. He has a MA in marketing.

The authors acknowledge the help and support provided to them by LGC Health Services in the preparation of this publication

This book is published by
Grosvenor House Publishing Ltd
28-30 High Street, Guildford, Surrey, GU1 3EL.
www.grosvenorhousepublishing.co.uk

A CIP record for this book
is available from the British Library

ISBN 978-1-78148-788-4

"all things are poison and nothing is without poison, only the dose permits something not to be poisonous"

Paracelsus
The father of toxicology
1493-1547

Document contents

Introduction

Sadly, generally a week does not pass without the issue of alcohol consumption or drug abuse appearing in the media. It is a fact that these issues are a part of our present day society. This has impacted on the approach of companies who recognise that society does not stop at a business's front door. An employee who is chemically dependent does not arrive at his/her workplace and miraculously switch off their problem until they leave for home. Unfortunately, the individual's problem will enter the workplace and can have a major impact on business performance.

Whilst the number of people who may develop a serious drug or alcohol problem may be small, approximately 2% of drug users and around 4% of regular drinkers, the potential negative effect upon companies can be enormous. The negative effects can include a rise in absenteeism, poor punctuality, decrease in productivity and an increase in workplace accidents.

Thus a question organisations must ask themselves is:

"What would be the impact on our business of a drug or alcohol related incident?"

- Damaged image?
- Client/customer confidence?
- Legal implications?
- Financial repercussions?

A (**2010 Home Office Crime Survey**) report stated that almost one in ten adults between 16 and 59 had used drugs in the past year. Figures showed that Britons were the biggest consumers of cocaine in Europe. Nearly a million people were estimated to have taken the drug in the previous year. About 12,000 people were being treated for their use of powdered cocaine.

It is estimated that British industry loses £800 million per year due to drug abuse related sickness (**National Treatment Agency**). Absenteeism caused by alcohol misuse is estimated to cost up to £6.4 billion per annum in lost productivity through increased absenteeism, unemployment and premature death (**Government's "Alcohol Harm Reduction Strategy for England", Prime Minister's Strategy Unit**).

This document has been developed to give organisations an overview of drug and alcohol issues and to act as an aid in the development of a drug and alcohol policy. It explains the relevant processes for screening and gives an insight into many of the issues that companies will face when introducing such policies.

Producing a policy.
What are you trying to achieve?

The policy is your formal statement of intention. It should clearly state the rules and procedures for dealing with the issues of substance misuse. It must be consistent with your other company employee guidelines and contracts. But try not to complicate issues.

You need to consider:

- Who does the policy cover? For example, some organisations differentiate between employees who carry out safety related tasks (sometimes referred to as "safety critical" tasks) and those who fulfil administrative roles.
- Your compliance with any legal requirements.
- Giving support to your managers and supervisors to deal with substance misuse in the workplace.
- Demonstrating "due diligence" with regard to health and safety.
- Establishing clear guidance for dealing with misconduct as a result of substance misuse.
- Raising awareness amongst employees to the potential effects of drugs and alcohol, alongside the potential impact upon individuals, in the workplace.

3

- Will the policy be supported by the introduction of a testing regime?

Not all organisations are the same size or operate in the same environment. Thus a company that operates in safety critical industries may have differing concerns (and sometimes differing legal requirements) from those in an office based environment. Therefore you need to consider the possible impact of a drug or alcohol related incident upon your particular organisation. Possible effects include:-

- Damaged image.
- Client customer confidence.
- Legal implications.
- Financial repercussions.

A major issue of the policy is whether it follows the principle of "carrot and stick"? This relates to whether or not you offer assistance to those employees who come forward voluntarily with drug or alcohol problems. However, this should be supported by a tough stance such that employees who are found to be in breach of the company's policy (which is normally established through a testing regime) may face dismissal from the company.

If offering support, then the policy should clearly state the nature and extent of support available from the company.

It is important that the policy clarifies what would be deemed inappropriate or unacceptable. Examples include:-

- Attempting to work whilst having alcohol and/or drugs in the system.
- Driving company vehicles whilst having alcohol and/or drugs in the system.
- Selling or possessing illegal substances.
- Sickness absence due to undisclosed drug and/or alcohol problems.

During the development stage it is vital to consult with employees and their representatives, including trade union officials. Consulting with your employees will not only ease a policy's introduction but will also reduce employees concerns thereby reducing the level of resistance.

The policy should support your company's commitment to health and safety, highlighting the potential dangers of substance misuse to employees and the impact on the organisation.

When dealing with the management of incidents and discipline you will need to clarify the responsibilities applying to staff, supervisors and managers. The document needs to explain the relevant processes and who should follow them.

If assistance is offered to an employee then the policy should provide the relevant information on where to seek advice and help.

Education can play an important part in enhancing the effectiveness of a policy. Thus it is essential to inform staff about the policy and how it will operate.

The company should also commit to the promotion of awareness in respect of the dangers of drugs and alcohol.

It is important to provide specific training for managers and supervisors so that they are confident in recognising the effects of drugs and alcohol within the workplace. Ultimately, it will be the frontline managers and supervisors who will oversee the operation of the policy. They will need to understand the reasons for its introduction, the processes that are to be introduced and the signs and symptoms of alcohol and drugs in affected individuals. It cannot be taken for granted that they are already very familiar with these things.

If a policy is to be supported by a testing regime, then a decision must be made on what tests will be adopted.

Some organisations have taken a zero tolerance approach with regard to the consumption of alcohol, thus minimising any safety risk. e.g.:

- Not to consume alcohol whilst at work, during breaks in the working day (including meal breaks spent away from the company premises) or if "on call" which might require the individual to work for the company at short notice.
- Neither to buy alcohol whilst at work nor to bring alcohol onto the company premises. ("Premises" also includes company vehicles).
- To limit consumption of alcohol prior to the commencement of work.

- To avoid consuming alcohol outside of work hours whilst wearing a company's uniform or other form of company identification.

When discussing alcohol a decision will need to be taken on the setting of a company "limit" for the testing process. Education should sit high on the company's agenda.

When considering your attitude to drugs a recommended approach would be to ensure that employees must:

- Not consume or use illegal drugs at any time so as to ensure they are not under the influence when reporting for work and/or carrying out work for the company whether on company premises or in company vehicles.
- Not to possess, store or sell illegal drugs on company premises or to bring the company into disrepute by being involved in such activities outside of work.

Employees may be required to inform managers if they are commenced on new treatments by health professionals. A policy should also cover over the counter remedies purchased in pharmacies.

It should be made very clear what constitutes a disciplinary matter in respect of drugs and alcohol. e.g.:

- The use of drugs (as defined by the Misuse of Drugs Act) during the working day.
- Working under the influence of drugs and alcohol.

- Being in possession of an illegal substance in the workplace.
- If testing is part of the policy, then an employee's failure to provide a sample must also be included as a disciplinary matter (In many policies a failure to provide a sample is treated as a fail unless there is a definite medical reason to explain why there is a problem in producing a sample).

Finally, the company should decide on its position with respect to agency workers, contractors' employees and suppliers. Due to their involvement with your organisation by working in (or visiting) your workplace, you may decide to require them also to have in place a policy and testing regime. Some organisations require that all external agencies working for them must indicate that their personnel have been tested as part of a formal testing regime for alcohol and drugs.

Top Tips

- *Set out why the policy is being introduced and what its objectives are.*
- *Make it clear who the policy covers.*
- *Talk to your employees at an early stage.*
- *Introduce a robust education programme for your managers, supervisors and trade union officials. Don't assume that employees know the risks of drug and alcohol in the workplace.*
- *Be clear on the principles of "carrot and stick" policies.*
- *If offering support to those who come forward admitting a problem, then state very clearly the extent to which you will give support.*
- *Decide how your policy will be supported. Will you be introducing a testing regime?*
- *Make very clear what constitutes a breach of the company's disciplinary processes.*
- *Ask for expert guidance at the development stage. Many anxious hours can be saved in the creation of a drugs and alcohol policy. Work with professionals who have the expertise in developing policies and introducing/running testing regimes.*

Plain speak

There a small number of widely used terms that you are likely to encounter when introducing a drugs and alcohol policy:-

Demonstrate due diligence. An employer must take all reasonable precautions to prevent injuries or accidents in the workplace. In order to exercise due diligence an employer must have a policy and plan to identify possible workplace hazards and to carry out the appropriate corrective actions to prevent accidents or injuries arising from these hazards.

Legally defensible.

- Will the policy, testing technique and all its associated processes withstand critical scrutiny by a tribunal or court of law?
- Is the use of the technique consistent with pro-fessionally accepted best practices?

A process referred to as legally defensible is one which has been through a legal process and successfully stood up to a legal challenge.

Chain of custody. Relates to the records kept on the sample through the entire process. The term refers to the ability to guarantee the identity and integrity of the specimen from collection through to the reporting of test results.

A secure chain of custody, good analytical techniques used by a laboratory to confirm the identity of any drugs present in a specimen and a strong policy will lead to the production of a "legally defensible" report.

One common term used in the chain of custody arena refers to the A and B samples or the laboratory and donor samples. When a sample collection is made a minimum of two tubes must be filled. These are called the A and the B samples. The A sample is selected for laboratory analysis, whilst the B sample is kept sealed and will only be used if the donor instructs the laboratory to do so. The only practical reason for the donor to request this is if they wish to contest the original findings.

Safety critical work. This term can cover many definitions. In several industries there are clear legal definitions. This is the case in the rail industry, for example. However, in other sectors "safety critical" is the definition that organisations place on various tasks carried out by employees. This can refer to physical tasks or those of a decision making process, all of which can impact on the safety of an individual and others. The operation of machinery or vehicles can sit high on the list of activities.

The Medical Review Officer (MRO) provides an impartial and independent view in determining if there is a legitimate medical explanation for selected positive results. The nature of the role dictates that the position is filled by a medical physician. The MRO will have a detailed knowledge of substances of abuse and will also have undergone appropriate training in the interpretation and evaluation of drug and alcohol testing results. The MRO will have the final say in evaluating the results from the laboratory in the light of declared information and will then make an informed decision on the final outcome. The MRO will often work in close relationship with the laboratory-based toxicologists. [A toxicologist specialises in the science of drugs, including their chemical structure, techniques of analysing drug compounds and the effects of drug use and abuse].

Top Tip

- *Always obtain clear definitions of phrases or terms.*

"What's our legal position?"

There are some specific pieces of legislation that will assist you in clarifying your responsibilities.

Misuse of Drugs Act 1971: This a key piece of UK legislation relating to the control and classification of drugs. The Act (and its subsequent amendments) sets down the penalties for possession and supply of various illegal drugs. Section 8 of the Act allows for the prosecution of 'occupiers of premises' who permit the supply of controlled drugs on their premises. Not taking reasonable action to prevent supply has been legally found to constitute 'permitting'- turning a blind eye is not an option.

Health and Safety at Work etc. Act 1974: This sets out the duty of care of employers towards employees in the workplace. Section 2 of the Act places a duty upon employers to provide a safe place of work for employees. Failure to deal with an employee who is under the influence of drugs or alcohol (and who may constitute a risk to other employees) may leave a business vulnerable to prosecution.

Management of Health and Safety at Work Regulations 1998: Regulation 3 places a duty upon the employer to make a suitable and sufficient assessment of the risks to health and safety of employees and others affected by their undertaking.

Common Law: This places a duty on the employer to take reasonable care of the health and safety of employees.

Road Traffic Act 1988: This sets out the offence of driving (or attempting to drive) a motor vehicle whilst unfit through drink or drugs. With regard to alcohol it sets the legal limit.

The Transport and Works Act 1992: This makes it a criminal offence for those classified as "safety critical" to be unfit through drink or drugs. Employers must have in place systems to demonstrate "all due diligence".

Railway and Transport Safety Act 2003: This brought maritime and airline crews in line with railway employees. However in the case of certain aviation employees the alcohol levels are more stringent than that of railway employees.

Corporate Manslaughter and Corporate Homicide Act 2007: This act sets out a specific offence for convicting an organisation where there is a gross failure in the way that activities are managed or organised thereby resulting in:

a) a person's death;
b) a gross breach of a relevant duty of care owed by the organisation to the deceased.

In England, Wales and Northern Ireland the offence is called corporate manslaughter. In Scotland it is termed corporate homicide.

Data Protection Act 1999: All health and medical information is classified as sensitive personal data under the terms of the Data Protection Act. All information surrounding possible drug or alcohol misuse must be handled securely and confidentially.

Human Rights Act 1998: Article 8 states that:-

- Everyone has the right to respect for his private and family life, his home and his correspondence.
- There shall be no interference by a public authority with the exercise of this right except such as is in accordance with the law and is necessary in a democratic society in the interests of national security, public safety or the economic well-being of the country for the prevention of disorder or crime, for the protection of health or morals, or for the protection of the rights and freedoms of others.

The first point in the Human Rights Act (1998) is often cited by individuals as to "what I do before I come to work has nothing to do with you!" However, the second point makes it pretty clear that if it impacts on health and safety it does matter!!

Top Tip

- *When in doubt always take a legal opinion.*

"To test or not to test?" That is the question

In the earlier chapters we discussed some of the most important points in the development of a robust drug and alcohol policy. Some organisations feel that the development of a written document is sufficient in making clear to its employees its position regarding the issues of drugs and alcohol in the workplace. Many companies will also introduce a screening/testing programme to support the policy. Today there is no accurate data of the number of employees subjected to testing in the UK. However, a survey in 2001 (**Chartered Institute of Personnel and Development**) indicated that only 18% of the companies with a drug and alcohol policy actually undertook workplace testing.

What are the main reasons that should be considered for introducing screening? We earlier recommended that an organisation should consider what impact a drugs or alcohol related incident might have on a business e.g.:-

- Damaged image?
- Client customer confidence?
- Legal implications?
- Financial repercussions?

Does the company believe that a written policy alone would be sufficient to reduce such risk? Or does the company require a robust testing regime to act as a deterrent to those who present themselves at the working place having consumed substances which could impair their workplace performance?

Top Tips

- *Complete a risk assessment.*
- *Examine the negative impact on business performance.*
- *Look at national and regional trends.*
- *Examine industry best practices.*

"First the man takes a drink; then the drink takes a drink; then the drink takes the man."

Japanese Proverb

"Can you blow into this please sir?" Testing for alcohol

Things have progressed from the days of the old "blow in a bag" method so often seen in police dramas. Today companies have the option of several different methods.

The most common methods are by analysing:

- **Breath**
- **Urine**
- **Blood**

Breath testing: The most common and well established method for alcohol testing is by the use of a breathalyser. The test uses a hand-held device which tests for the number of microgrammes of alcohol in 100 millilitres of breath and thus gives an almost instantaneous result. A printout is produced as a record of the result. If the reading is found to indicate a "positive" result then, following a prescribed waiting time, a further test is undertaken. The reading of a second test will be accepted as the result.

In adopting the use of a breath test the company must agree on its "limit" in terms of breaching the company's policy. In the UK several industries are covered by prescribed legal limits:-

- The Road Traffic Act   35 microgrammes of
                                alcohol in 100 millilitres
- The Transport at   35 microgrammes of
  Works Act 1992   alcohol in 100 millilitres
- The Railway and   9 microgrammes of
  Transport Safety   alcohol in 100 millilitres
  Act 2003   applies to aviation crews.

However, following the introduction of the Transport at Works Act the rail industry sought further medical advice. It was subsequently established that amounts of alcohol up to the higher limit outlined in the 1992 Act could still impair performance of safety critical tasks on the railway. Subsequently, a significantly lower limit was set as the industry prescribed standard. Today the rail standard is 13/14 microgrammes of alcohol in 100millilitres.

A company must be clear on the implications of its chosen prescribed limit for alcohol. Alongside setting its limit the organisation must have clear processes and procedures in place to deal with employees who register just below the company's prescribed limit. An employee whose level is 25 microgrammes, (where the prescribed limit is 35) will need some managerial input.

Urine testing: Indicates the presence of alcohol in a person's urinary system. It takes up to two hours for alcohol to show up in urine. It can assist in giving an historical overview for an individual and is thus generally used for pre-employment testing.

Blood alcohol testing: This is a very accurate method of testing. However, it is the most intrusive method and so is not generally recommended as the method of choice for the occupational testing arena. There is also the possible risk of needlestick injuries and the potential complications thereof to consider.

Top Tips

- *Breath test is the gold standard for employee testing of alcohol.*
- *Before setting your breath test limit seek advice regarding best practice. Just because a legal limit exists that does not mean it necessarily fits your business.*
- *Be clear what steps you will take with individuals that fail your limit.*
- *Be clear what steps you will take with individuals who fall just below the company's prescribed limit.*

Drug testing
"What am I looking for?"

So you have a policy and you have decided that you are going to introduce a testing regime. We all know about alcohol. It is easy to detect and we can smell it. But drugs? That's a different story. We have seen it on TV drama stories and we have probably heard of cannabis and cocaine. But what of the others? And do we really understand their effects? This is where the experts can give you informed guidance. The collection agency, working alongside laboratory colleagues (toxicologists), will be able to advise on a suitable panel of drugs for testing and their respective cut-off levels.

Drug testing cut-off levels are the minimum concentrations of drugs that must be present in a donor's specimen before a laboratory will report the drug test results as positive. This will also depend upon a number of factors, including the detection time, frequency of use, type of specimen, drug testing methods, age, state of health etc.....

A basic testing regime will typically screen for the following, commonly abused drugs :-

- Amphetamines (speed, meth, crank, ecstasy, meth-amphetamine)
- Cannabinoids (marijuana, hash)
- Cocaine (coke, crack)
- Opiates (heroin, morphine, opium, codeine)
- Benzodiazepines (temazepam, valium)

Further testing might also screen for some or all of:-

- Barbiturates
- Hallucinogens (LSD)
- Ketamine
- Phencyclidine (PCP)
- Methadone

Top Tips

- *Obtain clear guidance from your collection agency for advice on what constitutes best practice.*
- *If you are aware of a potential substance issue, then discuss.*

Drug testing methods

The most common methods for drug testing are:

- **Urine**
- **Oral fluid**
- **Blood**
- **Hair**

Urine drug testing: Is the most widely used method of testing. Although it has an element of intrusiveness the process is proven to be legally defensible. The normal process involves the sample being divided into different containers, being sealed under the requirements of a chain of custody regime and being sent to a laboratory for analysis. Negative results are returned within 24 to 48 hours. Urine testing is supported by ALL international guidelines.

More recently the introduction of "instant cups" or, to use their correct title, "Point of Collection Tests"/ "Point of Care Tests" (PoCTs) has been seen. They are screening tests that can be used on-site and can give a result in minutes. However, at present these tests have still not been "legally defended" and there are serious concerns because of the significant number of false positive and false negative results. They are also not supported by any international guidelines.

Oral fluid testing: Oral fluid collection devices come in many different forms. Some require the donor to rinse the mouth with a solution and then spit into a cup. Other methods rely on the inside of the mouth being wiped with a swab. Generally, samples can be collected easily and in virtually any environment.

One key disadvantage with oral fluid drug testing is its narrow detection window. Depending upon the rate of oral fluid produced by the donor, alongside the selection of drugs being tested for, the detection window can range from a few hours to a maximum of 24 hours. Another issue with oral fluid analysis is that problems can arise when a "B sample analysis" is required as not all laboratories are able to analyse the oral fluid from the large variety of devices used to collect oral fluid samples. Whereas there are well established and universal guidelines to support laboratory based urine testing, this is not the case for oral fluid testing. In fact, there are only limited guidelines for laboratory based oral fluid testing.

Blood testing: Is one of the most accurate methods of testing when considering impairment. However, it is very intrusive with the possible risk of needlestick injuries and the potential complications thereof.

Due mainly to their intrusiveness, blood drug tests are typically the least common method when testing for drugs.

Hair drug testing: Because of its long drug detection window hair testing can be useful for pre-employment testing. However, it is generally an expensive method.

European guidelines exist for the analysis of drugs in hair.

Hair testing is not normally a practice that is used in day to day screening. This method is more generally used in cases of long term drug abuse and in recovering addicts.

Top Tips

- *Select a test that is fit for purpose – don't overcomplicate.*
- *Select processes that are legally defensible - this could prevent hefty legal costs.*
- *Treat any considered use of PoCTs with a high degree of caution.*

Detection periods

To help with the decision on testing methods the following table is provided to give to a general overview of substances, testing methods and detection windows. The information is provided purely as a guide as detection times are dependent upon a large number of factors such as those discussed on page fourteen.

Substance	Urine	Hair	Oral fluid	Blood
Alcohol	Hours	Weeks to Months (depending on length of hair)	n/a	Hours
Amphetamines (including ecstasy)	1-3 days	Weeks to Months (depending on length of hair)	Up to 24hrs	Hours
Benzodiazepines	5 days*	Weeks to Months (depending on length of hair)	Up to 24hrs	Hours
Cannabis	5 days*	Weeks to Months (depending on length of hair)	Up to 24hrs	Hours
Cocaine	1-3 days	Weeks to Months (depending on length of hair)	Up to 24hrs	Hours
LSD	Hours	Weeks to Months (depending on length of hair)	n/a	Hours
Opiates	1-3 days	Weeks to Months (depending on length of hair)	Up to 24hrs	Hours
Methadone	1-3 days	Weeks to Months (depending on length of hair)	Up to 24hrs	Hours

* Chronic use can lead to considerably longer times
Karch M.D, S.B, 1997, Drug Abuse Handbook, page 777

When and why to test?

So you have decided that you are going to introduce testing into your organisation. There exist several screening processes to select from. In this part of the document we will explain the different types and how to use them.

Pre-employment - By introducing screening you can highlight drug misusers prior to employment. Both a breath alcohol and a drug test can be chosen. However, in some organisations only a drug test is selected, the alcohol being dealt with under the letter of introduction which explains a company's position on alcohol. Hence any individual turning up for an interview smelling of alcohol, may be deselected from the start. As one HR manager once said, it's an "intelligence test".

"For Cause" – The for cause test is introduced to cover all employees. It is used where there is reasonable suspicion that an employee is under the influence of drugs and/or alcohol. Employees will be removed from safety critical work and are supervised until the collection officer arrives. (Most collection agencies will offer a two hour arrival time).

"Post Incident" The "post incident" test takes place after a workplace incident has occurred where potential injury or loss of life could have, or has, occurred. It becomes is an integral part of the health and safety procedures of the company. (Again a two hour collection time is provided by the collection agency).

Random/Unannounced: The testing will generally occur without notice being given. Companies will set a minimum annual target of donors to be tested (e.g. 5 or 10%). It is highly recommended that the phrase used in policies should state that a **"minimum"** number of employees will be tested (e.g. "a minimum of 10% of employees will be tested").

By its very name, **"unannounced"** refers to a process whereby only a very restricted number of persons are aware that the testing agency will visit a site. In an ideal situation the company will appoint a "liaison" representative who will discuss with the collection company a regime for visits. The dates and times are kept confidential (including, where practical, even from the site manager or supervisor). The testers will thus turn up unannounced for the screening. This approach can greatly assist in the prevention of collusion occurring.

The process for random selection can raise some concerns with employees. It is thus important that the process is as transparent as possible. Many collection agencies have their own selection software that can be used to fairly select employees.

Monitoring: Relates to the scenario where an employee has returned from a treatment programme. An unannounced testing regime will be introduced for a designated period (normally 12 months). Such arrangements are usually introduced with the full acceptance and understanding of the employee.

Top Tips

- *Introduce pre-employment screening to reduce the potential of future issues.*
- *Set a minimum figure of tests for random/ unannounced testing (e.g. 5-10% of workforce).*
- *Be alert to any potential collusion amongst both managers and staff.*
- *Differentiate between "for cause" and "post incident" testing.*
- *If offering assistance to employees who have declared drug/alcohol problems then ensure that a monitoring regime is in place.*

APPENDICES

- A snapshot guide into drugs and some of their effects
- Reference guide for alcohol units
- Laboratory-based chain of custody drugs and alcohol testing versus on-site instantaneous point of care testing
- Example of a collection process
- Offering support

A. A snapshot guide into drugs and some of their effects

Drugs can be categorised into the following groups

1. Depressants	2. Stimulants
3. Opioids	4. Hallucinogens

1. Depressants

Types:

A. Alcohol
B. Sleeping pills
C. Tranquillisers

Effects:

Relaxation	Drowsiness	Disorientation
Delayed reaction	Sleep	Coma

Alcohol

Signs of use: People are different, tolerance levels are not the same

Smell (even vodka)	Slurring of speech	Repetitive speech
Obvious drunkenness	Loss of balance	

Dangers and effects of long-term use:

Obesity	Diabetes	"Drinkers nose and face"
Depression	Nerve damage/ clumsiness	Impaired memory
Stomach ulcers	Cirrhosis of liver(fatal)	Impotence
High blood pressure	Heart disease	Various cancers

Tranquillisers Tranx – Benzos – Valium - Temazies

Effects:

Fragile personality	Memory impaired	Slurring
Repeating themselves	Can't stay on the subject	Rambling

Dangers and effects of long-term use:

Rapid dependence in order to function	Prone to panic and to over-react to stress	Development of phobias
Loss of confidence		

2. Stimulants

Types

A. Caffeine
B. Amphetamines
C. Cocaine
D. Ecstasy (M.D.M.A)

Amphetamines - Speed – Whizz – Fast – Uppers – Billy

Cocaine/Crack – C – Coke – Charlie – Lady - Base – Freebase - Rock

Effects:

Increase in energy	Nothing is any trouble	Warm glow towards life
Manic talkativeness – all about themselves	Huge pupils	Chewing action
Dry mouth	No appetite	

Dangers and effects of long term use:

Paranoia	Psychosis	Looks like a skeleton
Rapid decay of teeth and nails	Loss of hair	Sores around the lips

Ecstasy - XTC - Dennis – MDMA -E- Doves – Edward – Disco - Biscuits

Signs of use:

Lots of energy	Warm feelings towards others	Manic dancing
Dilated pupils	Intense sweating	

Dangers and effects of long–term use:

Danger of heat – stroke and dehydration from dancing in packed areas	Paranoia etc.	Prolonged depression due to change in brain chemistry

3. Opioids

Types

A. **Heroin** – H – Junk – Jack –Skag-Smack –Gear – Harry - Horse
B. **Methadone**
C. **Morphine**
D. **Codeine**

Effects:

Relaxed	Laid-back manner	Pinpoint pupils
Itching on face	'Nodding out'	No perception of worries

Danger and effects long-term use:

Chronic unreliability	Failure to meet commitments	Thoughtless behaviour
Chronic loss of weight	Sores and track marks (injections)	Overdoses
Liver problems	Jaundice	Hepatitis
Deterioration of appearance	Chronic anxiety	Hopelessness

4. Hallucinogens

Types

- **LSD** - Stars – Acid – Sugar – Flash - Trips
- **Psylocibic mushrooms** –Magic mushrooms
- **Cannabis** - Skunk – Dope – Bush – Weed – Grass – Pot – Ganga – Hash – Wacky Backy

Effects of use:

Various (according to substances)	Cannabis often undetectable save for smell	Detached from reality
Preoccupied with odd things	Avoids hassle	Laughs at nothing

Dangers and effects of long-term use:

Isolation	Heavy thoughts	Depression
Can precipitate psychosis in already vulnerable individuals	Smoking cannabis significantly increase chances of mouth and throat cancer	

Alcoholism/Addiction

What is the difference between heavy usage and addiction?

In general terms heavy usage has some elements of personal control. The main difference is the absence of any meaningful control.

Alcoholism/Addiction can be characterised by the following:-

- Denial.
- Potential loss of employment may lead to attempts to cover up.
- Blackouts.
- Memory loss.
- Frequent drinking alone.
- Loss of interest in hobbies or pastimes.
- Frequent drink driving.
- Secretive drinking and hiding of consumption.
- Persistent remorse.
- Aggression when questioned about drinking.

- Repeated failure of attempts to control or stop.
- Mood swings/psychological problems/depression.

Alcoholism may lead to:-

- Progressive downhill illness, characterised by loss of control.
- Denial – brought on by shame, fear, guilt, confusion - will swear black is white!
- Manipulation – get others to bail them out, spouses, colleagues.

Top Tips

> - *Don't become part of the collusion – addicts may try to take emotional hostages.*
> - *Treatment depends on total abstinence and lots of help.*
> - *Be suspicious of those who say they are working their problem out. Success is rarely achieved through willpower alone.*

Alcohol Limits

Everyone is different, including their reactions to alcohol. Height, weight and gender are a few of the many factors which contribute to how alcohol affects you. Diet, exercise and tiredness can also play a part in how you feel when you drink.

The government advises that people should not regularly drink more than the daily unit guidelines of

3-4 units of alcohol for men (equivalent to a pint and a half of 4% beer) and 2-3 units of alcohol for women (equivalent to a 175 ml glass of wine). If you regularly drink more than this then please be aware of the associated health risks.

A Handy Reference Guide - Units of Alcohol

One unit of alcohol is roughly equivalent to:

- Half a pint of ordinary strength beer, lager of cider
- Half a 175ml glass of wine
- One 25ml pub measure of spirits

You can work out the exact number of units in a drink by multiplying the volume of the drink in millilitres (ml) by % alcohol by volume (ABV) as shown on cans and bottles. Divide the resulting numbers by 1,000.

For example the number of units in a 330ml bottle of lager with 5% ABV is:

$$\frac{ml \times \%vol}{1000} = units \qquad so \qquad \frac{330 \times 5}{1000} = 1.65 \; units$$

Here are some examples of units in some popular drinks:-

	Popular measure	Alcohol by volume (% ABV)	Units
Beer/Lager			
Caffreys Bitter	Pint (586ml)	4.8%	2.81
Fosters Lager	Pint (586ml)	4.0%	2.34
Guinness Stout	Pint (586ml)	4.1%	2.40
Heineken Lager	Pint (586ml)	3.4%	1.99
John Smiths Bitter	Pint (586ml)	4.0%	2.34
Kronenburg	Pint (586ml)	5.0%	2.93
Worthington Bitter	Pint (586ml)	3.8%	2.11
Stella Artois	Pint (586ml)	5.2%	3.05
Budweiser	330ml	5.0%	1.65
Becks	275ml	5.0%	1.38

Cider			
Strongbow	Pint (586ml)	5.3%	3.11
Woodpecker	Pint (586ml)	3.5%	2.05
Wine			

The alcohol strength of wine varies. As a general guide a 125ml glass of wine at 11% or 12% ABV contains around 1.5 units. A bottle of similar wine contains around 8 or 9 units

Spirit mixes			
Baileys	Glass (50ml)	17%	0.85
Smirnoff Ice	275ml	5.5%	1.51
Bacardi Breezers	275ml	5.4%	1.49
Archers Peach Schnapps	275ml	5.5%	1.51
Gin/Vodka/ Whisky/Brandy	Pub measure (25ml)	40%	1.00
Tia Maria	Pub measure (25ml)	26.5%	0.66
Tequila	Pub measure (25ml)	38%	0.95
Pimms	Pub measure (50ml)	25%	1.25
Low alcohol drinks			
Kaliber	Bottle (440ml)	0.05%	0.02
Swan light	Bottle (330ml)	0.33 not more than 1%	

Point of care testing kits (Urine screening)

Laboratory-based Chain of Custody Drugs and Alcohol Testing Versus On-site Instantaneous Point of Care Testing:

Comment	Laboratory-based Testing	Point of Care Testing
Chain of custody - Legally defensible in court?	Yes	No
Professionally interpreted results?	Yes	No
Recognised by UK, European and US Courts?	Yes, the laboratory Express Medicals use is UKAS registered.	No
Published data to defend results?	Yes	No
Reliable and scientifically backed results?	Yes	No

Comment	Laboratory-based Testing	Point of Care Testing
Quality controls in place?	Yes. Certified standards, quality controls, blank controls and expiry dates amongst many.	No. Expiry dates are of little significance where no other controls in place.
Possibility of incorrect results?	No	Yes
Interpretation Issues?	No	Interpretation not usually conducted by expert.
Are results "benchmarked?"	Yes. Urine sample testing equipment is calibrated on a regular basis i.e. every 50 sample tests.	Individual kits cannot be calibrated for accuracy.
Incorrect results?	No	Some kits have been known to give an incorrect result.
Implications surrounding objectivity of the collector?	None. Collection process is well established to avoid legal implications in this respect. Avoids spurious defence of a fail result.	Yes. With no established collections process, companies who carry out collections "in-house" may be subject to complaints/legal issues.

Comment	Laboratory-based Testing	Point of Care Testing
Sample available for further (contested result) testing?	Yes. A and B samples are collected and B sample is never opened. In the event of a fail the B sample is retained for 12 months to allow for independent testing.	No. There is no B sample.
Post supply of results support?	Yes. Our medical review officers, in conjunction with our partner laboratory, will be able to answer any question raised from a result supplied by Express Medicals Ltd.	No
Speed of results?	A "clean" sample i.e. no ingestion of medicinal or other substance in a sample then a report can be given the following working day. Can take up to five days to ascertain a fail.	Immediate, but does not differentiate levels of ingestion or some over-the-counter or prescribed medications.

Comment	Laboratory-based Testing	Point of Care Testing
Will medications affect the result?	Yes. However, a medical review officer will check the results against any medication(s) taken.	Yes. There are many over-the-counter and prescription medicines which will give a positive result.
Integrity of collection?	Yes. With an independent collector you will have the support of a proven system from collection to legal appeal (if appropriate).	No - If done in-house there is a possible issue of "conflict of interest."

Collection Process Example

Urine Drugs Test

- Facility prepared by collection agent.
- Establish a private interview area enabling the collection officer to interview the candidate and correctly package the sample.
- Toilet facility inspected, taps secured, windows are closed and any cleaning liquids removed to prevent adulteration of the sample.
- Coloured dye is added (e.g. a BLUE toilet disinfectant) to the toilet for each candidate.
- Donor is interviewed by collection agent.
- Confirm identification of donor.
- Chain of custody form completed donor asked to read and sign consent.
- Donor asked if they have taken any medication(s) during the previous 7-14 days.

Questions asked by agent designed to obtain medical information

- Do you take any prescribed medication on a regular basis?
- Have you taken any medication for and of the following ailments in the last 2 weeks?

- Headaches or other pains.
- Coughs, colds, flu or sore throat.
- Hay fever or other allergies.
- Hangovers.
- Upset stomach etc.....
- Have you taken any eye/ear/nasal drops?
- Attended a hospital, dentist, doctor or other medical practitioner during the past two weeks? If so, were any medications, including injections given?

Testing Process

- Donor asked to remove outer clothing and empty pockets. If possible place in a secure area.
- Donor asked to select a collection kit and is escorted to the toilet bringing sample equipment required.
- Collection officer must be present. However, all efforts must be made to allow the donor to give the sample in privacy, whilst at the same time minimising the opportunity for sample adulteration. Tester must be able to see the donor enter and leave the toilet.
- Donor is asked to remove a cup from the bag and provide a urine sample.
- After donor has provided sample, temperature and colour is checked.
- Fill the 3 sample tubes from the testing cup.*
- The procedure should take place with the donor present.
- The donor is asked to initial and date all seals.

---

*The use of three sample tubes refers to the collection process of LGC (Laboratory of Government Chemist). Other Laboratories may only use two tubes.

- In the presence of the donor the tamper evident seals are placed over the tubes, ensuring that the seals go completely over the caps and are firmly attached to both sides of the tubes.

Laboratory Process (LGC)

- The samples are received.
- First sample tested – if negative – all samples destroyed.
- If issue identified – second sample tested – A and "spare" B sample stored for one year – result given.
- If positive result given – A and "spare" B sample stored for one year – to enable challenge test to be carried out at alternative laboratory.

Results

- Generally negative results are issued within 24/48 hours.
- Results for samples in which issues are identified can take up to five days (This does not mean sample is necessarily positive).
- Positives are reviewed by a doctor before results are given.

Offering Support

If a company decides to support those employees who come forward in admitting a problem then the employer needs to ensure that individuals are professionally assessed in order to ensure that the correct treatment is offered. The company also needs to ensure that they have the correct support mechanisms in place when the employee returns to work after treatment has been completed.

A huge range of services offering differing types of assistance to those suffering from substance misuse are available and include the following:-

- **Statutory sector** – Part of the NHS – GP and community alcohol/drug teams etc...
- **Voluntary sector** – Can offer the same services as the NHS but often with a focus on counselling and advice services.
- **Private sector** – Here we have a wide range of services ranging from counselling to residential treatment.

General Practitioners: The majority of referrals to specialist services are made via GPs or mainstream NHS services. This has a number of advantages, especially because the GP will be aware of an individual's medical history and is normally well placed to monitor the situation.

Residential services: Residential treatment programmes are normally intended for heavily-dependent users. Although individual practices vary widely, residents are normally expected to have gone through a formal detoxification process prior to admission. Some centres may offer this prior to commencing the programme.

Self-help groups: Alcoholics Anonymous and Narcotics Anonymous are generally well known and act as an important support function for recovering addicts and their families/friends.

Substitute prescribing: For substances such as heroin there are substitutes which may be prescribed either by a GP or other specialist practitioners. A substitute like methadone can be prescribed to help gradually wean the user off drugs. There are many cases where individuals on methadone are able to effectively carry out work tasks without colleagues having any knowledge of their treatment. However, those who would normally carry out safety related tasks will need to be transferred to other tasks for the course of the treatment programme.

Treatment Programmes

Below are examples of potential treatments and possible timescales:

1. Drug or alcohol de-tox	3 weeks plus waiting time.
2. De-tox and day care	9 weeks plus waiting time.
3. Day care	4-6 weeks plus waiting time.
4. De-tox & residential	9 weeks plus waiting time.
5. Residential (no de-tox)	8 weeks plus waiting times.
6. Long stay	Up to 6 months.
7. Residential and secondary	Up to 9 months.

Overcoming a drug and/or alcohol problem is not easy and it is not unusual for an individual to relapse. This must always be considered by the employer. It is thus recommended that a monitoring testing programme be introduced. Employees who have been given the support of their employers will generally accept such a programme which is instigated as soon as an individual has been assessed as fit to resume work.

- Dr Dan Hegarty is a director of an occupational health company, Express Medicals Ltd.
- For details of the company's services, please visit www.expressmedicals.co.uk
- Mike Stallard is an advisor to Express Medicals Ltd
- LGC Health Sciences is a division of LGC Ltd (www.lgc.co.uk)